Wrestling with Words
Training Manual

Aaron Daffern

Wrestling with Words
Training Manual

Aaron Daffern

Aaron Daffern Consulting

2018

Copyright © 2018 by David Aaron Daffern

All rights reserved. This book or any portion thereof may not be reproduced or used in any manner whatsoever without the express written permission of the publisher except for the use of brief quotations in a book review or scholarly journal.

First Printing: 2018

ISBN-13: 978-0-9990241-5-7

Aaron Daffern Consulting

www.aarondaffern.com

Contents

1 Introduction 9

2 Prepare 11
    Jane Eyre by Charlotte Brontë 11
        Chapters 1-5 summary 11
        Chapter 6 excerpt 12
    Selecting Words 13
        4-Quadrant Vocabulary 14
        4-Quadrant Vocabulary with Scale 15
        Word Knowledge Scale 17

3 Present 21
    ABCs of Vocabulary Instruction 21
    Example 22
        Activate prior knowledge 22
        Bases/affixes 22
        Context clues 22
        Descriptive definition 23
        Examples/non-examples 23
        Friendly words/synonyms 23
        Grammar usage 23
    Practice 24

4 Place 29
    Free Association 29
    Semantic Maps 31
        Concept of definition map 31
        Synonym web 32
    Practice 33

5 Process 39
    Learning Styles 39
        Learning style inventory 40
        Scoring 40
    Mastery Tasks 41

- Frayer model 41
- Sentence completion 44
- Understanding Tasks 46
  - Solving analogies 46
  - Synonym feature analysis 48
- Interpersonal Tasks 49
  - Inside/outside circle 49
  - Roundtable 50
- Self-expressive Tasks 52
  - Keyword method 52
  - Opinion corners 55
- Complex Tasks 56
  - Response stems 56
  - Acrostics 59
  - Creating analogies 62

6 Play 69

- Classic Games 69
  - Charades 69
  - Draw me 70
  - Talk a mile a minute 70
  - Card games 70
  - Reflection 70
- Word Manipulation 71
  - Synonym strings 71
  - Word riddles 72
  - Categories 73
  - Word fluency 74

7 Plan 81

- Logistics 81
  - Primary grades 81
  - Sample schedules 82
- Implementation 83
  - My schedule 83

Chapter 6 excerpt continued (Jane Eyre) 84

Prepare 85

Present 87

Place 89

Process (basic) 91

Process (complex) 95

Play 97

Planning Matrix 98

1 Introduction

Vocabulary instruction has the potential to be extremely powerful. Word knowledge translates directly to reading comprehension and literacy serves as the base of education. Vocabulary has a significant effect on student understanding of not only written text but oral discussions as well. With that being said, it should not be an instructional afterthought. Instead, providing students with the opportunity to wrestle with words will nurture and even accelerate their intellectual growth. Powerful vocabulary instruction has five parts: prepare, present, place, process, and play.

The first part of any serious word study is preparation. All words are not created equal and chapter 2 explores two qualities that make certain terms worth examining: usefulness and importance. When words are highly useful, they have value beyond the text itself. They add to language development and expand general knowledge. Important words have high value within the text itself. Comprehension of the passage under consideration hinges on understanding important words. Chapter 2 looks at a 4-quadrant tool that teachers can use to evaluate terms by these two criteria. Additionally, students can use a word knowledge self-rating scale to reflect on prior knowledge and select interesting words to study.

The second part of wrestling with words is presenting or teaching them to students. As teachers come across potentially confusing terms during the course of instruction, there are seven angles, detailed in chapter 3, that they can use to teach them to students. Known as the ABCs of vocabulary instruction, the seven components begin with the first seven letters of the alphabet. Instead of repetitively defining each unknown term, the ABCs provide a menu to choose from so that direct instruction is both varied and complex. Learning new terms is greatly benefited from activating prior knowledge, bases/affixes, context clues, descriptive definitions, examples/non-examples, friendly words/synonyms, and even grammar usage.

Once unknown terms have been briefly explained using the ABCs of vocabulary instruction, the work shifts to the students. The third part of vocabulary instruction is placing the words in context. Looked at in chapter 4, students begin to understand word meanings when they associate new terms with existing semantic domain knowledge. A variety of semantic maps can be used, such as a synonym web or a concept of definition map, to help highlight the relationship between new and familiar words.

The fourth part of a powerful vocabulary program is processing. Students should spend ample time examining how words react to various contexts. Chapter 5 looks first at processing tasks through the lens of four major learning styles: mastery, understanding, self-expressive, and interpersonal. Applying word meanings from a variety of points of view and utilizing many cognitive approaches helps build well-rounded vocabulary knowledge. In addition to exploring basic processing tasks, chapter 5 also looks at complex processing tasks. Complex vocabulary activities rely more on generating responses than supplying correct responses from a word bank. Complex tasks naturally incorporate all four learning styles and stretch students to use vocabulary naturally and fluidly.

The fifth and final part of vocabulary instruction is playing with words. Chapter 6 provides many ideas on how word play can energize students and engage them in fun and meaningful tasks. A variety of word games exist that allow students to play with shades of meaning in a comfortable setting. When wrestling with words becomes associated with positive emotions, retention and familiarity increase dramatically.

Additionally, chapter 7 looks at several sample schedules that teachers can use to fit vocabulary instruction into their precious class time. Elementary language arts teachers that utilize centers or stations will have no difficulty integrating vocabulary instruction into their daily routines. Other teachers, however, that teach within smaller class periods or have other time constraints will need to plan how to best use their instructional minutes.

2 Prepare

Read the historical background and summary of the first five chapters of *Jane Eyre* below. Then read the excerpt from the beginning of chapter 6 on the following page. Highlight or underline any unknown terms that might be appropriate for vocabulary instruction. This novel is appropriate for typical 11th or 12th grade students.

Jane Eyre by Charlotte Brontë

Charlotte Brontë, born in Yorkshire, England in 1816, wrote *Jane Eyre* in 1847. As a critique of Victorian assumptions about gender and class, it stands as one of the most successful novels of its time. Many autobiographical elements weave their way throughout the story. One of the settings, Lowood School, is modeled after Cowan Bridge, a school for clergyman's daughters that Charlotte attended along with her sisters. The religious zealotry of Mr. Brocklehurst, the headmaster of Lowood School, mirrors that of Reverend Carus Wilson, the minster who ran Cowan Bridge. Additionally, the protagonist, Jane Eyre, becomes a governess – a position Charlotte held for two different families.

Chapters 1-5 summary

The novel opens at the home of the wealthy Reed family. The protagonist, Jane Eyre, is a young girl living with her aunt, Mrs. Reed, and her cousins, Eliza, Georgiana, and John. Mrs. Reed has forbidden Jane from playing with her cousins and John teases Jane, calling her a lowly orphan. Jane and John fight and Jane is blamed for the ruckus. She is banished to the red-room as punishment, the chamber in which her Uncle Reed died. She imagines that her uncle's ghost is in the room and becomes terror-stricken, finally fainting in exhaustion.

The family's apothecary, Mr. Lloyd, comes to treat Jane and suggests she be sent away to a school for girls. Jane overhears a conversation and learns that her mother was a member of the wealthy Reed family but was written out of the family will when she married Jane's father, a poor clergyman. Her parents both died from typhus, contracted while Jane's father cared for the poor. After months of waiting and mistreatment, Jane is finally told she can attend Lowood, an all-girls school run by Mr. Brocklehurst. Mrs. Reed warns him that Jane has a propensity for lying, which he vows to share with her teachers.

Soon after meeting Mr. Brocklehurst, Jane travels to Lowood alone. She is introduced to her classmates and learns the daily routine, filled from dawn to dinner. One of Jane's teachers, Miss Scatcherd, is unpleasant and particularly harsh in her treatment of Jane's new friend, Helen Burns.

Chapter 6 excerpt

The next day commenced as before, getting up and dressing by rushlight; but this morning we were obliged to dispense with the ceremony of washing; the water in the pitchers was frozen. A change had taken place in the weather the preceding evening, and a keen north-east wind, whistling through the crevices of our bedroom windows all night long, had made us shiver in our beds, and turned the contents of the ewers to ice.

Before the long hour and a half of prayers and Bible-reading was over, I felt ready to perish with cold. Breakfast-time came at last, and this morning the porridge was not burnt; the quality was eatable, the quantity small. How small my portion seemed! I wished it had been doubled.

In the course of the day I was enrolled a member of the fourth class, and regular tasks and occupations were assigned me: hitherto, I had only been a spectator of the proceedings at Lowood; I was now to become an actor therein. At first, being little accustomed to learn by heart, the lessons appeared to me both long and difficult; the frequent change from task to task, too, bewildered me; and I was glad when, about three o'clock in the afternoon, Miss Smith put into my hands a border of muslin two yards long, together with needle, thimble, &c., and sent me to sit in a quiet corner of the schoolroom, with directions to hem the same. At that hour most of the others were sewing likewise; but one class still stood round Miss Scatcherd's chair reading, and as all was quiet, the subject of their lessons could be heard, together with the manner in which each girl acquitted herself, and the animadversions or commendations of Miss Scatcherd on the performance. It was English history: among the readers I observed my acquaintance of the verandah: at the commencement of the lesson, her place had been at the top of the class, but for some error of pronunciation, or some inattention to stops, she was suddenly sent to the very bottom. Even in that obscure position, Miss Scatcherd continued to make her an object of constant notice: she was continually addressing to her such phrases as the following: "Burns" (such it seems was her name: the girls here were all called by their surnames, as boys are elsewhere), "Burns, you are standing on the side of your shoe; turn your toes out immediately." "Burns, you poke your chin most unpleasantly; draw it in." "Burns, I insist on your holding your head up; I will not have you before me in that attitude," &c. &c.

A chapter having been read through twice, the books were closed and the girls examined. The lesson had comprised part of the reign of Charles I, and there were sundry questions about tonnage and poundage and ship-money, which most of them appeared unable to answer; still, every little difficulty was solved instantly when it reached Burns: her memory seemed to have retained the substance of the whole lesson, and she was ready with answers on every point. I kept expecting that Miss Scatcherd would praise her attention; but, instead of that, she suddenly cried out "You dirty, disagreeable girl! you have never cleaned your nails this morning!"

Burns made no answer: I wondered at her silence. "Why," thought I, "does she not explain that she could neither clean her nails nor wash her face, as the water was frozen?"

My attention was now called off by Miss Smith desiring me to hold a skein of thread: while she was winding it, she talked to me from time to time, asking whether I had ever been at school before, whether I could mark, stitch, knit, &c.; till she dismissed me, I could not pursue my observations on Miss Scatcherd's movements. When I returned to my seat, that lady was just delivering an order of which I did not catch the import; but Burns immediately left the class, and going into the small inner room where the books were kept, returned in half a minute, carrying in her hand a bundle of twigs tied together at one end. This ominous tool she presented to Miss Scatcherd with a respectful curtesy; then she quietly, and without being told, unloosed her pinafore, and the teacher instantly and sharply inflicted on her neck a dozen strokes with the bunch of twigs. Not a tear rose to Burns' eye; and, while I paused from my sewing, because my fingers quivered at this spectacle with a sentiment of unavailing and impotent anger, not a feature of her pensive face altered its ordinary expression.

"Hardened girl!" exclaimed Miss Scatcherd; "nothing can correct you of your slatternly habits: carry the rod away."

Burns obeyed: I looked at her narrowly as she emerged from the book-closet; she was just putting back her handkerchief into her pocket, and the trace of a tear glistened on her thin cheek. (Public Domain)

Selecting Words

Which words did you identify for possible vocabulary instruction from the excerpt? Record them below.

_____
_____
_____
_____
_____
_____
_____

Work with your group to decide upon ten to twelve words that are good candidates for vocabulary instruction.

_____
_____
_____
_____
_____
_____
_____

Are there any unfamiliar words you did not include? Why did you exclude them?

_____
_____
_____
_____
_____
_____
_____

4-Quadrant Vocabulary

When preparing for vocabulary instruction, selecting the right words to teach is of utmost importance. Some words are too common or appear frequently enough in the selection that the meaning can be easily understood. Other words are obscure or highly technical, rarely used and/or limited to a narrow discipline.

Words worthy of study are those that rate high in two areas: importance and usefulness. Important words are essential for comprehension, either of the text or the unit of study. Not understanding important words will severely harm comprehension. Useful words, on the other hand, extend beyond the immediate lesson. They broaden knowledge and are used across the disciplines.

Looking at figure 1 (below), important words are measured on a continuum along the vertical axis. Useful words are measured along a continuum along the horizontal axis. Much like graphing on a coordinate plane in mathematics, words that rate high in importance fall on the upper part of the graph. Highly useful words fall on the right part of the graph. Putting these two dimensions together, words should be tiered for inclusion based on where they fall on the graph.

1. **High importance/high usefulness:** These words are instructional gold mines. They not only hold the key to understanding the passage under consideration, they also broaden general knowledge.
2. **High importance/low usefulness:** These words should be studied because they are important to the text or content at hand. They do not, however, appear frequently outside of the discipline.
3. **Low importance/high usefulness:** These words are not essential for comprehending the text or content. They do, though, provide wonderful opportunities to expand learning as they are a common part of language.
4. **Low importance/low usefulness:** These words should be ignored. They do not impact the overall meaning of the text and rarely appear in other disciplines. If necessary, they can be defined briefly with a definition but should not be the focus of learning.

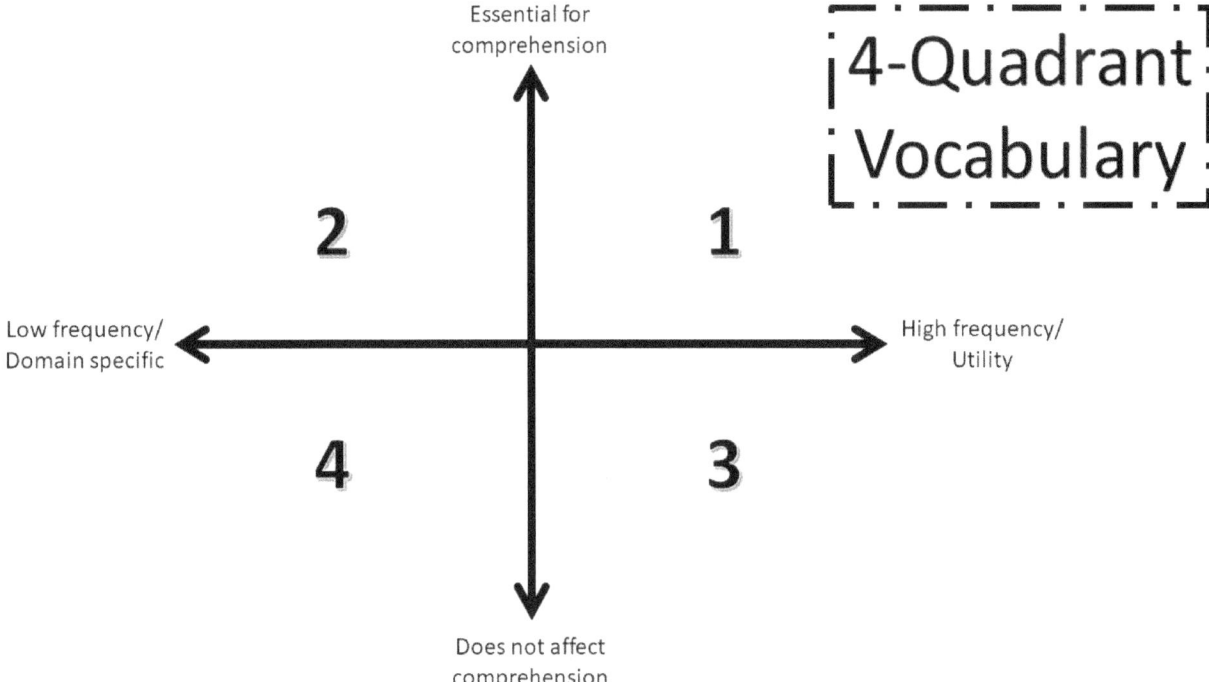

Figure 1: 4-quadrant vocabulary

4-Quadrant Vocabulary with Scale

Using either your own judgment or the questions in table 1 (next page), take a moment to rate each of the following words from the excerpt for importance and usefulness.

1. *commence*
2. *rushlight*
3. *crevice*
4. *ewer*
5. *muslin*
6. *animadversions*
7. *sundry*
8. *skein*
9. *ominous*
10. *pinafore*
11. *impotent*
12. *pensive*
13. *slatternly*
14. *glisten*

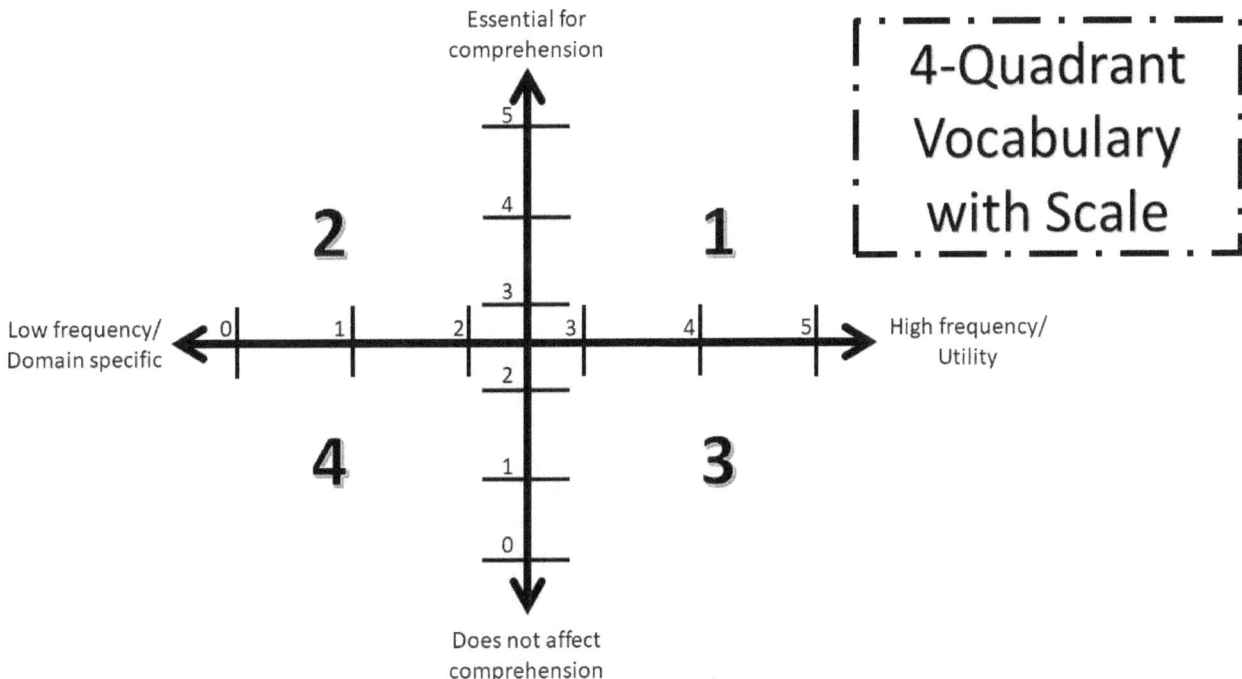

Figure 2: 4-quadrant vocabulary with scale

To use the questions in table 1, begin with the first word. Answer each question with either *yes* or *no*. Thus each word can have a minimum of 0 points and a maximum of 5 points. Record your totals in table 2 and rate each word as first, second, third, or fourth quadrant (Figure 2). The context for instruction is an 11th or 12th grade English language arts class.

Table 1: Questions for 4-Quadrant vocabulary with scale

Usefulness (horizontal axis)	Importance (vertical axis)
1. Are the students likely to encounter this word in other texts?	1. Is the word essential to the reading selection or unit of study?
2. Does the word relate to another topic in the classroom?	2. Will the reader not understand a major idea or concept without a good understanding of the word?
3. Is the word commonly used outside of the selection or theme?	3. Does the word play a role in communicating the meaning of the context in which it is used?
4. Is the word representative of a family of words important for learning in general?	4. Is the word or phrase representative of a concept the students will need to know?
5. Is this a word that will heighten students' enthusiasm for word learning?	5. Does the word bring clarity or specificity to the text or situation?

Table 2: Usefulness and importance matrix

Word	Usefulness (0-5)	Importance (0-5)	Quadrant (1-4)
commence			
rushlight			
crevice			
ewer			
muslin			
animadversions			
sundry			
skein			
ominous			
pinafore			
impotent			
pensive			
slatternly			
glisten			

Word Knowledge Scale

Another part of selecting words for study is asking students to rate their knowledge of potential terms on a scale from 1 to 4. If students have no understanding of a word, they would give it a rank of one. If they have at least heard it but can only vaguely guess at its meaning, it would receive a rank of two.

Words that students think they know, at least at a basic level, receive a rank of three. The final rank, four, is reserved for terms that students are very comfortable with. They not only know what it means, they can use it in self-generated sentences and various contexts.

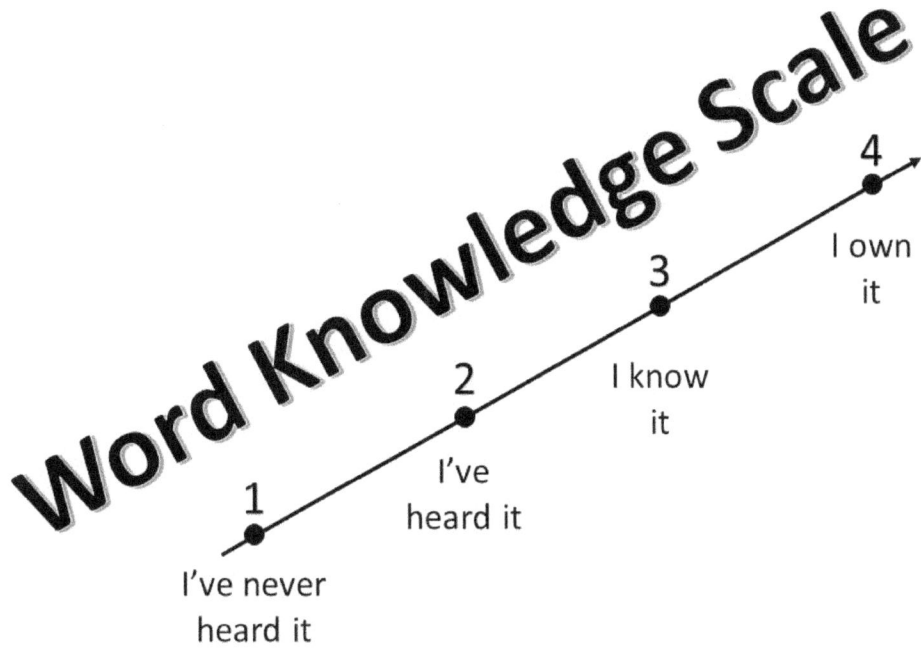

Figure 3: Word knowledge scale

Take a moment to reflect on your knowledge of the ten terms below. Give each word a rating based on your understanding before this training began.

These ratings have no bearing on where the words fell on the 4-quadrant vocabulary.

Word	Rating (1-4)	Word	Rating (1-4)
commence		muslin	
crevice		ominous	
ewer		pensive	
impotent		slatternly	
glisten		sundry	

Notes

Notes

Notes

3 Present

How teachers introduce new words as they are encountered during reading is an important part of vocabulary instruction. There are seven angles from which to present new words, each starting with the first seven letters of the alphabet.

ABCs of Vocabulary Instruction

The first component teachers can utilize is activating prior knowledge. Helping students access what they already know about a concept is vital. This helps students associate the term with existing knowledge and greatly increases recall. Rather than starting the discussion with the new word as the object, teachers can generally speak about the concept without mentioning the word itself. Once students have begun to get a picture of the new idea, the new vocabulary term can be presented to give students a label for a concept they are beginning to explore.

The second angle is exploring any bases or affixes. When examining vocabulary for various word parts, a few questions can be asked. Are there any prefixes or suffixes that help add meaning to the word? Is there a root word within the term that can be used to explore other related words? How will knowledge of these word parts help students analyze other related words?

Third, some words are embedded within a paragraph that provides clues to their meanings. When appropriate, discussing words in a rich context is more effective and natural than simply providing them with a definition. This further reinforces the fact that words derive much of their meanings from their surroundings. Sometimes words take on different connotations based on how they are used in various contexts.

The fourth method, definition, is one that is usually employed to explain new terms. How the definition is crafted, though, can do much to help or hinder understanding. Sometimes definitions from the dictionary or glossary include unknown terms and muddy rather than clear up the word's meaning. Since words are used to define other words, a key to remember is that the definition needs to be in language that is easy to understand. The purpose is to convey meaning and that requires that the words used to define the unknown term are themselves understood. Instead of a tightly-controlled definition that is sparse and technical, definitions should be given in a more conversational style first before the technical definition is explored.

Fifth, teachers can relate new terms to everyday concepts through the use of examples. Deeper connections are formed when students explore the relationships between ideas. Additionally, the use of non-examples adds richness to the vocabulary words. Sometimes a new idea can be identified as much by what it's unlike as what it's like.

The sixth direction educators can utilize to explain new words is through the use of synonyms. Sometimes called *friendly words* in the primary grades, synonyms are important for a variety of reasons. If the concept represented by the vocabulary term is known to students, it's easier for them to apply a new label to that unknown topic if they can relate it to a similar word. Synonyms also provide an opportunity to explore the nuances of language. Though they are similar to the target terms, there will inevitably be differences that can be highlighted.

Finally, grammar usage provides another window into the meaning of vocabulary words. Knowing which part of speech a word belongs to (e.g., noun, adverb, etc.) helps explains its usage in the text. Sometimes the word origin can provide additional information about the term. Words evolve and change over time and these permutations heighten word-learning interest and fill seemingly ordinary words with historical depth.

Example

The following is a sample of the ABCs of vocabulary instruction being used with the term *antebellum*. Though this includes all seven angles, most words can be satisfactorily introduced with just a few.

Activate prior knowledge

"We've been studying the U.S. Civil War for a few days now. We know that this event in the 19th century was one of the watershed events in our nation's history. It marks a division in our country's timeline, especially as it concerns the culture and heritage of the South. Before the war, slavery, large plantations, and gallant chivalry dominated Southern culture. Afterwards, the devastation of the war, the Emancipation Proclamation, and Reconstruction politics forever changed the lives of Southerners.

"When we discuss U.S. history in the South, it's very important to note whether the topic we are talking about took place before or after the war. There is a term that we can use to quickly note if something took place before the Civil War. One vocabulary word we will be looking at this week is *antebellum*. Even though it can be used to describe something that happened before any war, it usually refers to Southern life before the U.S. Civil War."

Bases/affixes

"If you look at the word *antebellum*, you'll notice that it has a prefix *ante-*. That's a good term to know because it means 'before' like the prefix 'pre-.'

"Another word with the same prefix is *antechamber*. Taking what you know of *ante-*, you can guess that an *antechamber* is something before a room. In fact, an *antechamber* is a small room that serves as a gateway into a larger room or reception area.

"Finally, if you've ever played a game of poker, you know that before you play each round some or all of the players have to put a small amount of chips into the pot. This is called the *ante* because it happens before anyone sees their cards."

Context clues

"Let's examine the sentence in the book that has one of our vocabulary words. 'The *antebellum* era is often associated with slavery, conflict, and sprawling Southern plantations.' There are several clues in the sentence that could help us define the word *antebellum* even if we hadn't already discussed it.

"First we see that *antebellum* is used as an adjective to describe era. This lets us know that *antebellum* refers to a specific time period in our history. The fact that it is often associated with slavery lets me know that the era happened before slavery was abolished after the Civil War.

"When it says that the *antebellum* era is also associated with conflict, that also makes me think that the Civil War is involved since that is the largest conflict in our history that involved slavery. Finally, Southern plantations being associated with the *antebellum* era lets us determine the geographic location associated with the word *antebellum* – the Southern states."

Descriptive definition

"*Antebellum* is a descriptive term that places something or someone in a particular period in history. Most of the time it's used, it refers to something that happened before the American Civil War. Though it can be used to describe something that happened before any war, it typically is reserved for this particular conflict.

"What's more, over the years it has been mostly used to refer to something in the Southern states before the Civil War. Even though Northern, Western, and Southern states had unique cultures, architecture, and customs before the Civil War, *antebellum*, which literally means "before the war," usually refers to Southern society before 1861."

Examples/non-examples

"Let's look at a few examples of *antebellum* to see how it's used. This picture of a plantation house from Georgia, built in the 1820s, can be described as an *antebellum* plantation because it's typical of Southern architecture before the Civil War.

"This picture of a dress can also be described as an *antebellum* dress because it was fashionable in the decade before the Civil War. More importantly, the style was seen a lot in balls and dances held in Southern states during that time, another requirement for use of the term *antebellum*.

"This picture of a New England shipyard could not be described as *antebellum*, however. Even though you see it is dated 1834, well before the Civil War, its location, the North, is not where our term *antebellum* usually refers to. If this shipyard happened to be in South Carolina or Virginia, then we could then call it *antebellum*."

Friendly words/synonyms

"Another way to think of the term *antebellum* is to remember the synonym *prewar*. We know that the prefix *pre-* means 'before' so if something is *prewar* that means it occurred before a war.

"One difference to keep in mind, however, is that *prewar* can be used as a general term. It doesn't refer to a particular war or geographic location. *Antebellum*, on the other hand, usually refers to the South before the Civil War."

Grammar usage

"One interesting thing about our term *antebellum* is that it is a direct translation from Latin. The word is made up of two Latin words – *ante*, which means 'before', and *bellum*, which means 'war.' Our word *antebellum* is literally the Latin phrase for 'before the war.'

"If you've ever heard of the word *bellicose* it's related to the Latin word *bellum*. *Bellicose* means 'easily angered' or 'ready to fight' because it comes from the Latin word for war.

"In English, *antebellum* is used as an adjective. It describes things or events that happened before the Civil War. A plantation or a military uniform can be described as *antebellum*."

Practice

Listen to the following examples. As you hear one of the ABCs being used, check the appropriate box.

The ABCs of Vocabulary Instruction
Activate prior knowledge
Bases/affixes
Context clues
Descriptive definition
Examples/non-examples
Friendly words/synonyms
Grammar usage

Figure 4: ABCs of vocabulary instruction

Example 1: *animadversions*
- o **A**ctivate prior knowledge
- o **B**ases/affixes
- o **C**ontext clues
- o **D**escriptive definition
- o **E**xamples/non-examples
- o **F**riendly words/synonyms
- o **G**rammar usage

_____
_____

Example 2: *pinafore*
- o **A**ctivate prior knowledge
- o **B**ases/affixes
- o **C**ontext clues
- o **D**escriptive definition
- o **E**xamples/non-examples
- o **F**riendly words/synonyms
- o **G**rammar usage

_____
_____

Work with your color group to select one of the following words to present. Try to include at least 3 of the ABCs in your presentation. Every group member should be comfortable with the presentation.

ewer   *muslin*   *pensive*   *slatternly*   *sundry*

_____
_____
_____
_____
_____
_____
_____

Regroup with your shape group. Listen to each presentation and identify which ABCs were used.

Word: _____
- **A**ctivate prior knowledge
- **B**ases/affixes
- **C**ontext clues
- **D**escriptive definition
- **E**xamples/non-examples
- **F**riendly words/synonyms
- **G**rammar usage

Word: _____
- **A**ctivate prior knowledge
- **B**ases/affixes
- **C**ontext clues
- **D**escriptive definition
- **E**xamples/non-examples
- **F**riendly words/synonyms
- **G**rammar usage

Word: _____
- **A**ctivate prior knowledge
- **B**ases/affixes
- **C**ontext clues
- **D**escriptive definition
- **E**xamples/non-examples
- **F**riendly words/synonyms
- **G**rammar usage

Word: _____
- **A**ctivate prior knowledge
- **B**ases/affixes
- **C**ontext clues
- **D**escriptive definition
- **E**xamples/non-examples
- **F**riendly words/synonyms
- **G**rammar usage

Regroup with your number group. Reflect on what you've learned about the ABCs and record your thoughts.

_____
_____
_____
_____
_____
_____

Notes

Notes

Notes

4 Place

After teachers have presented unknown terms to students using the ABCs of vocabulary instruction, the students must shoulder the mental load of making meaning of new words. The first task students should engage in is placing target terms within existing semantic knowledge systems. Two methods that students can use to place words in context are free association and semantic maps.

Free Association

Work with a partner and write down as many words or phrases you can think of that are associated with the target term. These associations are based on your own prior knowledge, not a dictionary or thesaurus.

Word: _____

_____
_____
_____
_____
_____
_____

Word: _____

_____
_____
_____
_____
_____
_____

Create a group of people (4-8). Like the game Hot Potato, you are going to have a limited time to associate words or phrases with the vocabulary word displayed on the screen. When the timer goes off, the last person who spoke must justify why his/her association is related to the target term. After each round, take a few moments and write down words or phrases that were shared.

Word: _____

_____
_____
_____
_____
_____
_____
_____

Word: _____

_____
_____
_____
_____
_____
_____
_____

Word: _____

_____
_____
_____
_____
_____
_____
_____

Three Strikes and You're Down: Everyone stands up to share words or phrases aloud. If someone shares a word or phrase that you have written down, cross it out. Sit down when you have either shared a word or phrase or when you have crossed out 3 items.

Semantic Maps

Another useful tool for placing words within known word systems is building specific thought organizers, called semantic maps, that explore these relationships. Look at the examples below of a concept of definition map and a synonym web.

Concept of definition map

Using this map, students display hierarchical, categorical, and semantic information. Related to a word under consideration, students answer three questions. What is it? What is it like? What are some examples?

The first category seeks to define the term in student-friendly words. If studying the word *mollusk*, science students would define it as an invertebrate with a soft, unsegmented body that lives in damp or aquatic habitats.

The second category asks students to provide characteristics of the term to better understand it. Again referring to *mollusk*, students would brainstorm various descriptions of mollusks they know from reading and prior knowledge. They might produce phrases such as *usually has a shell*, *muscular foot*, and *mantle*.

Finally, students produce examples of the target term in order to place it within their network of existing knowledge. Instead of a completely unknown term, the purpose of the last category is to firmly relate the new term with prior experience. Students might give such examples as snails, squids, clams, and octopuses.

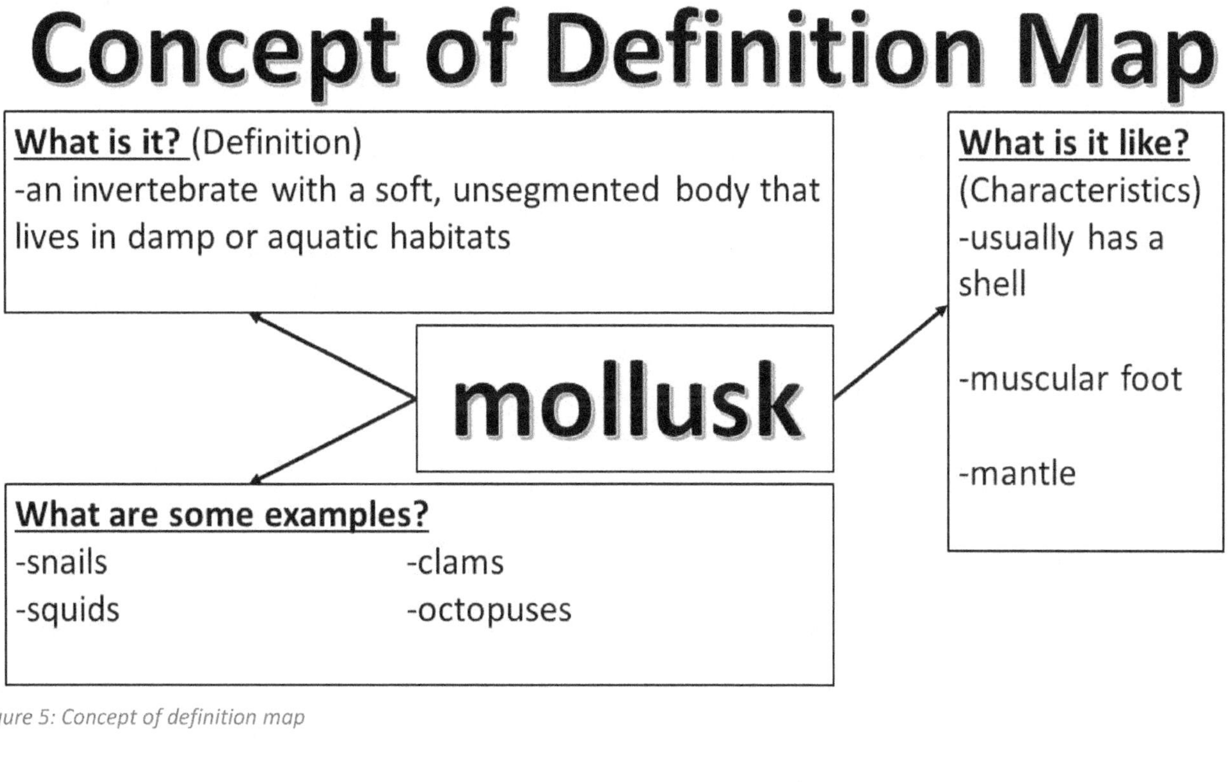

Concept of Definition Map

What is it? (Definition)
- an invertebrate with a soft, unsegmented body that lives in damp or aquatic habitats

mollusk

What is it like? (Characteristics)
- usually has a shell
- muscular foot
- mantle

What are some examples?
- snails
- squids
- clams
- octopuses

Figure 5: Concept of definition map

_____
_____
_____
_____
_____
_____

Synonym web

One of the simplest semantic maps for students to create is a synonym web. Students work together to come up with as many synonyms of a target word as they can. They then build a web that groups synonyms based on shades of meaning for more complex words. For teachers of language arts, examining alternatives for the word *said* is a common practice.

Creating a synonym web provides a great opportunity to introduce and practice thesaurus skills. Most students will know only a few synonyms for a word, if any, and be able to produce only a simple web on their own. They should utilize print or online resources to generate multiple synonyms and then work to classify the terms into categories based on similarities.

The figure below is a fairly complex web. Until students become familiar with the process, their webs might only have one or two branches. In addition, it would be prudent to include a discard pile for words that do not fit neatly onto the web. Trying to wrestle every word into a category can result in warping the meaning of words beyond their true definitions.

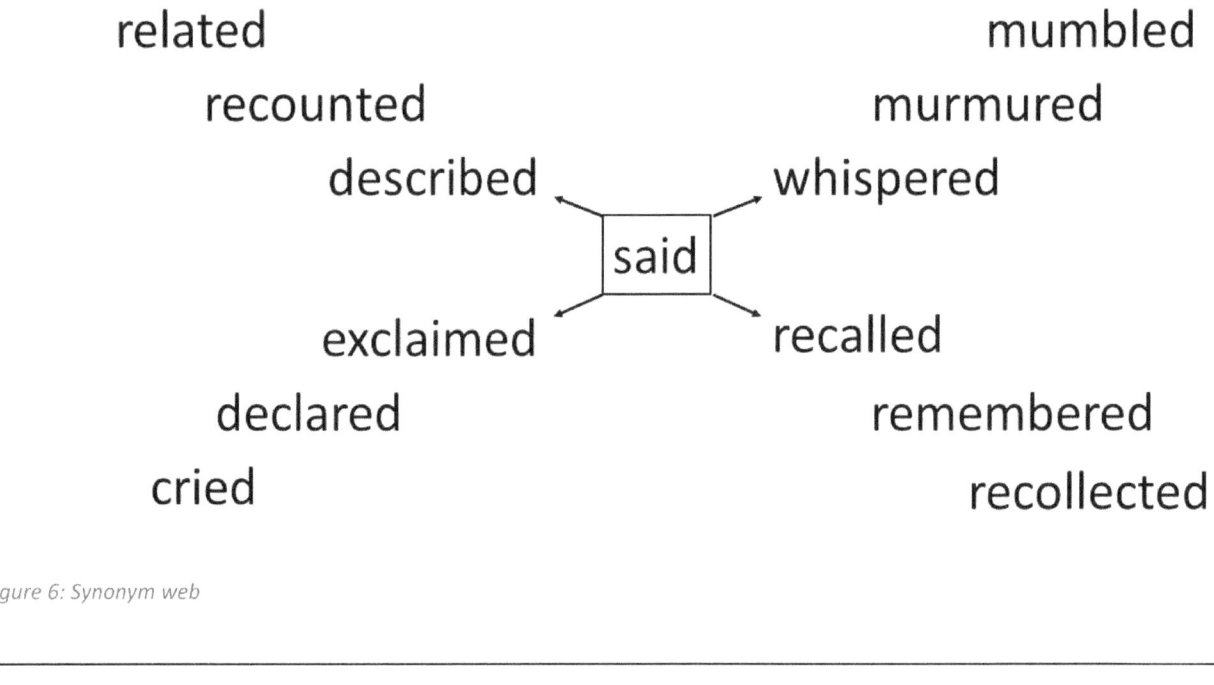

Figure 6: Synonym web

_____
_____
_____
_____
_____
_____

Practice

Use these pages to draw a concept of definition map or synonym web of a word from the list below.

commence *crevice* *ewer* *pensive*

Notes

Notes

Notes

5 Process

Process tasks come in two different forms. Basic tasks require students to apply their understanding of vocabulary words within various contexts. The structure of basic tasks is largely created by the teacher and the student's responsibility is to supply the correct term. Complex tasks, on the other hand, are much more open-ended. Rather than answering a question or filling in a blank, students generate responses with self-selected terms. Answers can vary greatly and tasks are more open to interpretation.

A method used to organize process tasks is through the lens of learning styles. Basic tasks are grouped by the primary learning style associated with the thought process or activity required of the student. Complex tasks, however, are designed to integrate all four learning styles throughout the task.

Learning Styles

Mastery learners do best when remembering and summarizing. They enjoy clear sequences, expanding competence, and measurable success. These learners prefer tasks such as to-do lists and memorization. For the most part, the traditional education system is built for these types of learners. Of all the students that populate classrooms across the country, mastery learners are the most likely to enjoy fill-in-the-blank worksheets. Mastery learners are most concerned with questions like, "What?" They want to know the correct answer and what they need to do to show their competence.

Understanding learners, however, prefer using reason and logic. Mysteries that invoke their curiosity and opportunities to analyze and debate are highly motivational. These learners prefer to know why something works rather than simply performing a task or remembering a fact. They relish the opportunity to explore the nuances of word meanings and enjoy analyzing context and grammar usage. Understanding learners are more driven by questions like, "Why?" Instead of simply knowing the solution, they seek to know why those solutions work.

The third type of learning style is interpersonal and these students are driven by questions like, "Who?" Interpersonal learners thrive while utilizing their social prowess. They learn best when relating the content to themselves and others. Teams, cooperative learning, and even coaching motivate them through the energy they derive from relationships. These learners would rather read a story about someone in history than perusing a dusty history textbook.

Finally, self-expressive learners prefer to use their imagination and creativity. They are constantly asking "What if?" and trying new ideas out. Imagery, metaphors, and patterns motivate them to express their individuality and originality. These learners not only want to know how something works, they want to tweak it and make it their own.

Take the learning style inventory on the next page to explore your own learning preferences. Additional copies and versions of the inventory can be found online at AaronDaffern.com/inventories.

Learning style inventory

Answer each statement with either Strongly Disagree (SD), Disagree (D), Agree (A), or Strongly Agree (SA).

_____ 1. I like creative activities and problems that aren't multiple-choice.

_____ 2. I learn best by being close with the teacher.

_____ 3. I want to use logic and reasoning to solve problems.

_____ 4. I have difficulty with questions that aren't multiple-choice.

_____ 5. I like cooperative learning and role play.

_____ 6. I learn best by being challenged and explaining my answer.

_____ 7. I want to use my imagination.

_____ 8. I want to learn useful information and procedures.

_____ 9. I learn best by showing my thinking in unique ways.

_____ 10. I enjoy discussions and group activities.

_____ 11. I have difficulty when there is too much group work.

_____ 12. I learn best from lectures and practice problems.

_____ 13. I enjoy brainstorming and finding multiple solutions.

_____ 14. I want to learn about things that affect people's lives.

_____ 15. I enjoy getting help that improves my performance.

_____ 16. I enjoy asking, "Why?"

_____ 17. I have difficulty with independent work or tasks that don't connect to my life.

_____ 18. I like drills and when the teacher demonstrates how to do something.

_____ 19. I have difficulty with memorization and a lot of practice problems.

_____ 20. I like debates and investigations.

Scoring

SD = 1, D = 2, A = 3, SA = 4

Learning Style	Item Numbers	Learning Style	Item Numbers
Mastery total: ____/20	(4, 8, 12, 15, 18)	Self-expressive total: ____/20	(1, 7, 9, 13, 19)
Understanding total: ____/20	(3, 6, 11, 16, 20)	Interpersonal total: ____/20	(2, 5, 10, 14, 17)

Additional copies and versions of the inventory can be found online at AaronDaffern.com/inventories.

Mastery Tasks

Tasks that focus on the mastery learning style seek to concretely define new words and place them firmly within semantic domains. These tasks can sometimes resemble traditional worksheets as they, in part, utilize fill-in-the-blank style questions.

Frayer model

Frayer models are a multi-dimensional approach that help students connect prior knowledge to target vocabulary by utilizing various types of connections. In the traditional Frayer model, students split a piece of notebook or journal paper into four quadrants. After writing the vocabulary word in the middle, students write a definition in the upper left-hand quadrant. This definition should be in the student's own words rather than a sterile dictionary definition. For struggling students, teachers can provide a definition with simplified language.

The upper right-hand quadrant is where students record characteristics of the target term. They should focus on features that help students identify the word and what distinguishes it from other related words. The lower left-hand quadrant is for examples while the lower right-hand quadrant is for non-examples. They can be synonyms (examples) or antonyms (non-examples), correct or incorrect applications, or even illustrations. The non-examples should stand in contrast to the target word rather than being something completely unrelated and random.

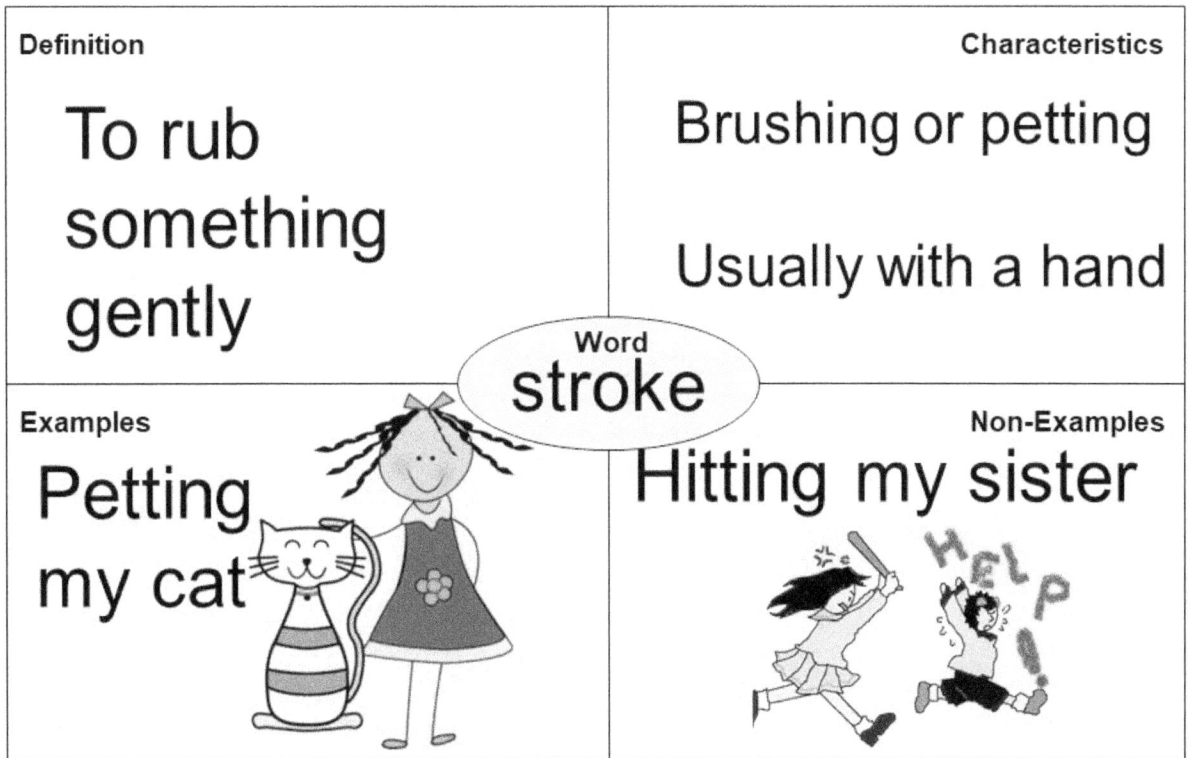

Figure 7: Frayer model

Use these pages to draw a Frayer model of a word from the list below.

glisten   *impotent*   *ominous*   *sundry*

Sentence completion

Another mastery learning task is sentence completion. This technique can be approached using two different methods, both of which are important. First, teachers can give students a sentence that provides definitional context for a vocabulary term and ask students to supply the correct word. Conversely, teachers can provide a vocabulary term within context and ask students to finish the sentence using descriptive terms.

Word bank

commence   *crevice*   *ewer*   *impotent*   *glisten*
muslin   *ominous*   *pensive* *slatternly*   *sundry*

Sentence completion set 1

1. She reached for the _____ to refill the fish tank with water.

2. They hurried to find their seats since the show was about to _____.

3. The mouse ran into the _____ to escape the jaws of the tomcat.

4. Tears made her cheeks _____ as she said goodbye to her grandmother for last time.

5. He felt _____ as the larger boys threw his backpack's contents all over the sidewalk.

6. The _____ thunderclouds on the horizon threatened to delay the start of the game.

7. She enjoyed finding unique buys at yard sale amidst its _____ tables and racks.

8. The restaurant hostess looked contemptuously at the _____ attire of the teenagers.

Sentence completion set 2

1. A strip of *muslin* can be used _____
   _____.

2. You might feel *pensive* when _____
   _____.

3. I know a test is about to *commence* when _____
   _____.

4. A situation in which I felt *impotent* was when _____
   _____.

5. A *crevice* might form when _____
_____.

6. A *ewer* is useful for _____
_____.

7. When something is said to *glisten*, it can be described as _____
_____.

8. Someone who sounds *ominous* would say, "_____
_____."

9. If your brother's room was *slatternly*, it would look like _____
_____.

10. If there were *sundry* cereal boxes on a store shelf, you would see _____
_____.

Reflection: How did making a Frayer model and utilizing sentence completion support mastery learners?

_____
_____
_____
_____
_____
_____

Understanding Tasks

Understanding tasks are more focused on digging beneath the surface of word meanings. They seek to provide depth to target terms by exploring their relationships with other words, specifically synonyms. As students play with the nuances of word meanings within various contexts, they add to their growing understanding of their definitions.

Solving analogies

Analogous thinking is a solid processing task that asks students to identify and interpret the relationships between words. A key part of activity is understanding the relating factor that ties the two words together. When considering analogies, most adults tend to think about the kinds of problems given to high school students on the SAT test. For example, a typical question is set up like this:

Choose the answer that best matches the analogy: **walk:legs**

   A. *gleam:eyes*

   B. *chew:mouth*

   C. *dress:hem*

   D. *cover:book*

   E. *grind:nose*

The key to finding the answer is to analyze the relationship between the original pair. Students at a young age can be trained to evaluate analogies if shown how to verbalize the relationships between words. Using the example above, students should place the two words in a sentence that explains how they are related. They might come up with something akin to "you walk with your legs."

Taking that simple phrase, students then substitute the other pairs and evaluate their reasonableness. Using this method, they can quickly see that the best answer is B because "you chew with your mouth." For students to solve analogies, teachers should set them up with increasingly difficult and varied relationships. Different types of analogous relationships can be found in the table below.

Table 3: Analogy relationships

Type	Relationship	Example
Synonym	is similar to	happy:glad
Antonym	is the opposite of	anger:joy
Part to Whole	is a part of	hand:body
Category	is a type of	dog:mammal
Object-Function	is used to	scale:weigh
Person-Action	does/performs	boxer:fights
Cause-Effect	is a cause of	poison oak:rash

Solve the following analogies using the word bank below.

Word bank

commence	crevice	ewer	impotent	glisten
muslin	ominous	pensive	slatternly	sundry

Solving analogies

1. angry:irate::thoughtful:_____

2. first:last::neatly:_____

3. coffee:Folgers::fabric:_____

4. buzzer:end::bell:_____

5. milk:carton::water:_____

6. mountain:valley::closure:_____

7. mirror:reflect::raindrop:_____

8. sage:foolish::dictator:_____

Solving analogies challenge

Use the two unused words from the word bank above to create your own analogies.

9. _____:_____::_____:_____

10. _____:_____::_____:_____

47

Synonym feature analysis

Synonym feature analysis, sometimes called semantic feature analysis, requires students to delve deep into the nuances between word meanings. The primary goal is to add texture to target word meanings by differentiating between denotations (e.g., literal meanings) and connotations (e.g., suggested meanings) of various synonyms. By evaluating related words, students add depth and complexity to their understanding of vocabulary words.

One method of analyzing synonyms is to use a sample sentence. To begin with, a single vocabulary word should be chosen, either by the teacher or the student, as the subject of analysis. Then, either by brainstorming, the use of a thesaurus, or both, a list of synonyms should be created. Keep in mind that the synonyms should be words that students know and are comfortable with.

The next part is the creation of the sample sentence. It should be fairly simple yet descriptive of the vocabulary word. Students will read the sample sentence multiple times, each time substituting a synonym for the vocabulary word and discussing how the connotative interpretations change with each new word.

Word: *glisten*
Synonyms: flicker, gleam, glimmer, glint, glitter, glow, shine, sparkle, twinkle

1. The trace of a tear *glistened* on her thin cheek.
2. The trace of a tear *flickered* on her thin cheek.
3. The trace of a tear *gleamed* on her thin cheek.
4. The trace of a tear *glimmered* on her thin cheek.
5. The trace of a tear *glinted* on her thin cheek.
6. The trace of a tear *glittered* on her thin cheek.
7. The trace of a tear *glowed* on her thin cheek.
8. The trace of a tear *shined* on her thin cheek.
9. The trace of a tear *sparkled* on her thin cheek.
10. The trace of a tear *twinkled* on her thin cheek.

Questions to discuss:

- How did the sentences change with each new word?
- Which synonyms were closest in meaning to *glisten*? Farthest? Why?
- Can the synonyms be categorized by attribute/description (e.g., descriptive of a flame, mirror, etc.)?
- How do these synonyms add to your understanding of *glisten*?

Interpersonal Tasks

Learners whose primary learning style is interpersonal get much satisfaction from working with others. Rather than toiling independently to solve problems, or exploring the intricacies of word nuances, interpersonal tasks emphasize relational learning. They leverage social interactions to maximize vocabulary instruction.

Inside/outside circle

A technique that can be utilized to encourage student interactions is an inside/outside circle. To easily facilitate productive conversations, students form two concentric circles. A quick way to form the circles is to have the entire class form one large circle and number off starting at one. The students with the odd numbers will form the outer circle. The students with the even numbers will take one step inward and turn around to form the inner circle.

With the two circles formed, students should make an inner-outer pair. It is at this point that the teacher should direct the students to respond to vocabulary-related questions with their partners. They can give synonyms to a certain word, provide a descriptive definition, or generate real-word examples.

After each partner has responded, the teacher will direct either the inner or outer circle to rotate in a certain direction. For example, the teacher could tell the inner circle to move two places to the left or the outer circle to move three places to the right. Once one of the circles has moved, the teacher can ask another question or give another prompt for students to respond to with a new partner.

Form an inside/outside circle. Respond to the questions/statements about the words below.

Word bank

| commence | crevice | ewer | impotent | glisten |
| muslin | ominous | pensive | slatternly | sundry |

1. Select a word that is an adjective and use it in a sentence.

2. Which word was the least familiar to you at the beginning of the day? What do you know about it now?

3. Which word are you most likely to use in everyday conversation? Why?

4. Which word are you least likely to use in everyday conversation? Why?

5. Select a word that is a noun and use it in a sentence.

6. Ask a question using two vocabulary words.

7. Make a statement using three vocabulary words.

8. Which word were you most familiar with at the beginning of the day? What else have you learned about it?

9. Which word is most likely to be used in a doctor's office? Why?

10. Which word is most likely to be used in an auto shop? Why?

Roundtable

For teachers that want to include a multi-faceted approach to word study, roundtable is a great strategy to incorporate. In groups of four, each student folds a piece of paper into four quadrants. They each then fold a triangle in the corner of the paper with two folds. When unfolded, it opens up so that is looks similar to a Frayer model but with a diamond in the middle (Figure 8).

There are many different variations of this collaborative technique that teachers can use to encourage students to process vocabulary words. One method is to assign four words to each group and have each student choose a different word. Students then write down their thoughts or give examples of the word in one of the quadrants.

After a short time, students rotate their papers and add their thoughts about a different word on a new paper. They should read what has already been shared and attempt to add to those thoughts rather than repeating them. When the papers have rotated three times, they return to the owner with all four quadrants filled. Students then use the central diamond to write a statement that synthesizes everyone's thoughts. If students have questions about what someone else wrote, they can ask for clarification.

An alternate form of this method is to assign one word each group. After students fold their papers, they label the four quadrants like a Frayer model. Students fill in one quadrant of their choice for the target word and then rotate the papers. After each rotation, students fill in a different quadrant of their choice. If possible, they should choose a new quadrant to fill out so that they are not completing the same section (e.g., examples) for four consecutive papers. After the papers have been returned, students once again write a synthesis statement in the central diamond.

Figure 8: Roundtable

Use this page to complete a Roundtable with one of the words below. Each member in your group should choose a different word.

ewer	impotent	muslin
ominous	slatternly	sundry

Word: _____

Self-expressive Tasks

Self-expressive learners enjoy working in creative ways, manipulating words, images, and even ideas as they make something new. The more open-ended the task, the greater the level of engagement for these students. They disdain filling-in-the-blanks but instead prefer clean paper and a chance to shine.

Keyword method

One of the earliest and most researched methods for growing student vocabulary involves the manipulation of language. Also known as the mnemonic method, the keyword method uses both auditory and visual cues to enhance the learning of the word and its meanings. Students choose a familiar word or term that either lies within or closely resembles a part of the target word. This keyword is then illustrated to connect the keyword with the target word's meaning.

An example from elementary mathematics is the term *parallel*, which refers to lines that are the same distance apart and never intersect (Figure 9). The keyword for *parallel* would be its similarity to the phrase "pair of elves." Building on that, students can draw two parallel lines, include two elves, and write an understandable definition.

Figure 9: Keyword method

This method works well for some students because of how our memories work. It encodes information in multiple areas of the brain (i.e., visual, auditory, semantic) and greatly increases the chances of recall. While it does not necessarily provide deep analysis of words, it does allow self-expressive learners to explore their creativity. Instead of memorizing bland definitions, students will thrive with the opportunity to be creative.

Use these pages to create a Keyword Method representation of any of the vocabulary words listed below. The representation should be related to the vocabulary term through some type of auditory or visual cue. Also include a brief student-friendly definition.

Word bank

| commence | crevice | ewer | impotent | glisten |
| muslin | ominous | pensive | slatternly | sundry |

Opinion corners

This strategy asks students to evaluate statements concerning vocabulary terms and justify their reasoning. Opinion corners works best if each corner of the classroom is labeled either Always Agree, Sometimes Agree, Sometimes Disagree, or Always Disagree. If the layout of the room prohibits this, tables or various sections of the room can be labeled instead. Using the list of vocabulary words, students should respond to various declarative statements created by the teacher.

The students then will have to evaluate their response to teacher statements. They move to the corner that most closely corresponds to their opinion (i.e., Always Agree, Sometimes Agree, Sometimes Disagree, or Always Disagree). When all students have chosen their corners, the students confer with those that have similar beliefs. They discuss their reasoning and work together to share their justification with the class.

For those students in either extreme corner (i.e., Always Agree or Always Disagree), their purpose is to anticipate and plan for arguments dissuading them from their opinion. The two more central positions (i.e., Sometimes Agree or Sometimes Disagree) should seek to find fault in the opinions of the more extreme positions. These students are looking for examples to disprove an all-or-nothing opinion.

For this strategy to work, students need to be able to think outside the box, form cogent arguments, and know how to disagree in a respectful manner. As thoughts are shared with the class, students should be encouraged to change groups if they hear a compelling argument. Movement should be celebrated and the rationale for changing should be shared with the class. Instead of right or wrong answers, students work to hone their persuasive skills and learn how to have a respectful dialogue.

Evaluate each statement. Move to the corner that best corresponds to your opinion: Always Agree, Sometimes Agree, Sometimes Disagree, or Always Disagree.

Sample statements

1. Wearing a garment of *muslin* makes you appear *slatternly*.

2. *Crevices* are *ominous*.

3. Leaving a filled *ewer* next to your bed overnight will cause it to *glisten*.

4. People with *sundry* abilities do not feel *impotent*.

5. Athletes feel *pensive* right before the game *commences*.

6. *Muslin* can be used to create *sundry* items that soothe you when you feel *pensive*.

7. If there is no indoor plumbing, you should keep a *ewer* in a *crevice* to help *commence* hand washing.

8. One cannot feel *ominous*, *impotent*, and *slatternly* at the same time.

Complex Tasks

While basic (comprehension) tasks require students to evaluate and/or supply various vocabulary words, complex (generative) tasks are much more open-ended. These activities provoke students to engineer their own novel responses. Whereas the previous tasks sorted themselves by a single learning style, the following complex tasks are multi-faceted and incorporate all four learning styles.

One thought to keep in mind is that complex tasks are not necessarily more valuable than basic tasks. Instead, they demand a different type of thought pattern and should be used progressively. Students must first comprehend a word in a variety of ways (basic tasks) before they can use it independently to generate personal responses (complex tasks).

Response stems

A low-prep complex processing task that teachers can use is called response stems. Students take the beginning of sentences that target a particular word and complete them on their own. This can be done verbally or can be written down in vocabulary journals. Regardless of the method used to interact with response stems, the conversations that accompany the task are critical. Response stems are similar in makeup to sentence completion (mastery tasks). The difference lies in the rubric component (Table 4) of response stems and the possibility for largely varied responses.

Good response stems should target specific characteristics or senses. For example, ask students where something would take place or what they would do in a certain situation. Students can also complete a response stem with what they would say, feel, or even hear in response to a word. As with most open-ended tasks, they require a strong rubric to guide student responses. The use of a posted rubric provides reflective feedback for students and allows them a clear path toward improvement.

While simple sentences will successfully satisfy the requirements of this task, students should be encouraged to expand their writing to multiple sentences to fully flesh out their thoughts. Students should respond to the stems and then evaluate their own work using a rubric like the one on the following page. With enough practice, students can begin to craft detailed sentences or even paragraphs in response to a simple response stem.

The correct frame of mind for students to embody during this task is not one of completion but of explanation. Their goal is not to simply fulfill the task requirements but to expand their response to the fullest extent possible. With quality response stems, the possibilities are endless.

Mastery learners will benefit most from using the rubric. With something as open-ended as response stems, students who value growing their competence need structure. Using a rubric allows for these students to take the vagueness of a subjective task and give it some order.

Understanding learners, on the other hand, will be most drawn to level 3 and level 4 responses. They will relish the opportunity to show their comprehension of the word by generating sentences that are complex and informative. Their responses might be the most perceptive and nuanced in the class.

Interpersonal learners would benefit from working with a partner after the responses have been generated. In addition to a self-assessment using the rubric, some students would gain much from getting feedback from a peer. If the original sentence does not rank high enough on the rubric, they can work collaboratively to improve their response.

Finally, self-expressive learners will benefit most from the open-ended nature of the task. While understanding learners might deliver the deepest responses, these learners will most likely generate the most creative. A task like this allows them to think outside the box rather than hemming them in with worksheets and fill-in-the-blank assignments.

Table 4: Response Stem Rubric

Response Stem Rubric

Level	Description	Example
0	The response does not explain what the word means.	When I feel *disagreeable* I go to my room.
1	The response somewhat explains what the word means.	When I feel *disagreeable* I am angry.
2	The response explains what the word means.	When I feel *disagreeable* I am in a bad mood and no one wants to be around me.
3	The response fully explains what the word means with an example.	When I feel *disagreeable* I am unpleasant and don't enjoy things. If my friend suggests something to do, I say, "That's boring."
4	The response fully explains what the word means using multiple examples or perspectives.	When I feel *disagreeable* I snap at people for no reason. No idea is good enough and people usually avoid me. It's like I have a rain cloud over my head.

Response stems

1. My mother feels *pensive* when _____.

2. I look *slatternly* when _____.

3. A *crevice* is formed when _____

_____

_____.

4. My father sounded *ominous* when _____

_____

_____.

5. I knew the movie was about to *commence* when _____

_____

_____.

6. *Muslin* can be used in many ways, including _____

_____

_____.

7. The little girl, feeling *impotent*, said, " _____

_____

_____.

Acrostics

Students can also generate deep and meaningful interpretations of vocabulary words by creating acrostics. An acrostic, put simply, is a set of words, phrases, or sentences that revolve around a central word. Each letter of the word is used in a word or phrase to describe the term itself. While simple to explain and fairly common even in elementary grades, acrostics allow for many permutations and levels of support. Simple acrostics (Figure 10) use the first letter in the target word to stand for the first letter in multiple words that each describe the word under consideration.

Acrostic sentences (Figure 11), on the other hand, utilize the same structure but attempt to form a sentence or series of sentences describing the target word. Rather than each letter of the target word standing alone, acrostic sentences should be read in one fluid reading as you would a paragraph.

Finally, some students might struggle with the creation of either simple acrostics or acrostic sentences. A modified version of typical acrostics (Figure 12) allows students to use any letter in the descriptive words to match up to the letters of the target word. This adjustment works both for simple acrostics and acrostic sentences.

Regardless of the type of acrostics students work on, they should be encouraged to explore their creativity in a way that is comfortable to them. To ease students in the acrostic making process, ready access to a thesaurus, either print or online, should be available.

Simple Acrostic
Sad
Out of sorts
Remorse
Regret
Oppressed
Worry

Figure 10: Simple acrostic

Acrostic Sentence
Don't just
Exclaim, "I don't like it."
Some things deserve no
Pity or sympathy.
Irate feelings of resentment
Serve to show your attitude toward
Everything you truly loathe.

Figure 11: Acrostic sentence

Mastery learners will be drawn more to the simple acrostic with its clear layout and no-nonsense function. Though some might view it as more difficult than a modified acrostic, mastery learners will appreciate the simplicity of its design.

Understanding learners like to explore why things are true rather than just learning cold facts. They will enjoy the symmetry of using a word as a structure for defining itself. Understanding learners will most likely gravitate toward acrostic sentences as they seek to explain their target words with in-depth examples.

Interpersonal learners would obviously enjoy working with a group or partner. However, they are also drawn to stories, real or fictional, and relate well to characters. Their acrostic sentences might read more as a narrative than as a definition.

Self-expressive learners like to think expansively and any of these types of acrostics would appeal to them. Of all the learning styles, self-expressive learners would probably find the most elegance in the modified acrostic whereas the mastery learners would find it too chaotic.

Modified Acrostic
ele**G**ant
limbe**R**
be**A**utiful
deli**C**ate
Exquisite
grace**F**ul
s**U**pple
Lithe

Figure 12: Modified acrostic

Use these pages to create acrostics with of any of the vocabulary words listed below. Try to create two different types of acrostics (one per page).

Word bank

commence	*crevice*	*ewer*	*impotent*	*glisten*
muslin	*ominous*	*pensive*	*slatternly*	*sundry*

Creating analogies

While students can solve analogies as a level two processing task, generating analogies requires an entirely different set of thought processes. While constructing analogies around target vocabulary words, students should keep in mind the limits of the analogies. Building analogies helps students take an active role in learning. It creates conceptual bridges between what is known and what they are trying to learn.

Rather than simple analogies, though, students should work to create elaborate analogies. Elaborate analogies help students more accurately assess their own understanding of target terms. They provide students with personally relevant points of reference that enables them to evaluate their knowledge.

These analogies also serve as a self-diagnostic tool that fosters metacognitive thinking. They help create a mental framework for a word or concept and any related terms. Additionally, elaborate analogies increase students' sense of relevancy for the term or topic.

For students to create elaborate analogies, they must consider the vocabulary term and its characteristics. Words best suited for elaborate analogies are those that describe an action or a process. Target words, then, can be included in larger phrases or put into action to make them more accessible.

A previously-made semantic map, such as a concept of definition map (chapter 4) or a Frayer model (chapter 5), might help students fully examine the term. The goal is to find something similar to the target term that is familiar to the student. Students will utilize these two concepts to create the analogy.

First, students will identify the key features of the target word and the familiar concept. They will describe similarities between the two and show where the analogy breaks down (i.e., major differences). Finally, they will draw conclusions about any major ideas gleaned from comparing the word with the analogy.

Students can follow the six steps below to present their elaborate analogies, either orally or in written form:
1. Introduce the word to be studied
2. Review a familiar concept that will serve in the analogy
3. Identify relevant features of the vocabulary word and the analog concept
4. Explain what both concepts have in common
5. Indicate differences that cause the analogy to break down
6. Draw conclusions about major ideas that other students should remember about the word

Creating analogies involves multiple processes that lend themselves to the four major learning styles. The six steps described above will serve as a road map for mastery learners. They'll provide point-by-point instructions for successfully completing the task.

Understanding learners will enjoy exploring the similarities and differences between the word and the analog concept. They will probe deep in their examination of the related concepts and find hidden truths that other students might overlook.

Interpersonal learners, on the other hand, will find pleasure in choosing the analog concept for comparison. The ability to select something that is personally relevant to them will help them evaluate the target word more closely.

Finally, self-expressive learners will thrive with the fluid nature of this task. With the analog concept being open to choice and interpretation, they will make the most of their creativity.

See the example below for a student's created analogy about the word *joyously*.

Heather finished creating her elaborate analogy and shared it with her table partner. "The word I am studying is joyously. It's an adverb used to describe when something is done with great happiness or excitement. It reminds me of hitting the game-winning shot in basketball. Both the word joyously and hitting the game-winning shot involve feelings of enjoyment. They aren't always the same, though. You can do something joyously without winning. Maybe you learn you passed your test or you got to see your favorite movie on opening night. You should remember that the word joyously can be used to describe when something happens that you feel super excited about, like hitting the game-winning shot."

Use these pages to create an analogy with of any of the vocabulary words listed below.

Word bank

| commence | crevice | ewer | impotent | glisten |
| muslin | ominous | pensive | slatternly | sundry |

Notes

Notes

Notes

6 Play

Who says that vocabulary instruction needs to be tedious? The best type of learning happens when students are having so much fun that they don't even realize how hard their minds are working. A simple way to ditch boring worksheets and boost the energy level in the classroom is to encourage students to play with words. It not only serves as an integral part of initial vocabulary instruction, it also serves as a powerful tool for reviewing previously learned words.

Word play should not be seen as something to do when the *real* work of vocabulary instruction is finished. Instead, it is a motivating and important component of a word-rich environment. Word play cannot be done passively but instead requires students to actively participate. It requires students to reflect metacognitively on word parts and contexts. Additionally, word play promotes curiosity in children as they develop an appreciation of word study.

Playing with words, as a component of a rich vocabulary program, develops word meanings in multiple domains. Designed to be done with others, it plays to the natural strengths of interpersonal learners. Within the larger descriptive category of word play lies many types of semantic manipulation, such as punning and joking. Overall, playing with words develops phonological, morphological, and syntactic awareness in students.

Classic Games

Many ways in which students can play with words are known to most educators and even some students. These classic games require little to no preparation and can be repeated endlessly with ever-changing word lists.

Charades

Many students will be familiar with the idea of charades, or acting out words, though the term itself might be unfamiliar. There are a few different ways that students can interact with words playing charades. In the traditional setup, students work together in small groups. One person acts out the word silently while the group tries to guess what is being represented. This can be done either competitively, where points are kept and teams battle against each other to guess the most words, or in a more relaxed manner.

Another form of this can be accessed quickly by the teacher using a whole-class approach. The teacher asks the students to stand next to their desks and act out words called out by the teacher. Rather than guessing what word is being demonstrated, the students hear the word and then try to show it with their actions. This will open up many possibilities for unique portrayals to start class conversations. Teachers should look for ideal or unique demonstrations and ask students for the rationale behind their creative choices.

Draw me

Similar to the popular game Pictionary, Draw Me asks students to visually represent words with original drawings. The customary way to play the game is similar to charades, in which small groups either work together or compete to guess what words are being drawn.

Additionally, students can work in pairs to play Draw Me. Each pair would have a stack of vocabulary cards and each student would pick a card. At the same time, each partner would spend about one minute drawing their vocabulary word and then switch papers. After each student guesses what was drawn, the students talk briefly about why they drew what they did. It's these conversations that take place about vocabulary that have the greatest power to cement the words into long-term memory.

Talk a mile a minute

This game requires students to use oral language and precision to describe words. In the game, one person from a pair or a small group is designated the Talker. The Talker has one minute to attempt to describe a list of words and have the other students guess as many as they can. When the first word has been guessed, the Talker moves on to the next word until the minute is up.

What makes this challenging is that the Talker cannot use the word itself or any rhyming words as clues. Instead, the Talker must define, describe, or use context to place the words in the mind of the other students. To make it more challenging, teachers can list a few synonyms next to the target words that may not be used, similar to the game Taboo.

Card games

Many different card games, such as those based on Go Fish, Old Maid, or Memory Match, emphasize the semantic relationships between words. Using a pairing principle, students work to find matches between vocabulary words and other related terms.

The options for matching words are numerous. For a game such as Memory Match, students can work with a partner to pair up either vocabulary words with definitions or synonyms. For games that require sets of cards, sometimes called books, students can work to create a set of four cards: the vocabulary word, a synonym, a definition, and a symbol or picture.

Alternately, students can work together to match words with antonyms or find matching cloze sentences. When using games that require more than one match to each vocabulary word, it would be wise to keep an answer key with the card games so disputes can be settled quickly. Students can even create many of these card games themselves.

Reflection

After you've had a chance to play a classic game, reflect on the experience. How can these games be used in your classroom to support word learning? Which ones do you think your students would most enjoy? Why?

_____

_____

_____

_____

Word Manipulation

Another facet of playing with words involves examining how their meanings change in varying contexts. This can come by exploring synonyms, creating puns, or classifying terms by certain attributes.

Synonym strings

Students can work together to build connected sets of synonyms. Facilitated either with simple brainstorming or with the use of a thesaurus, students not only look for the relationships between words but also take note of the slight variations as the strings become longer.

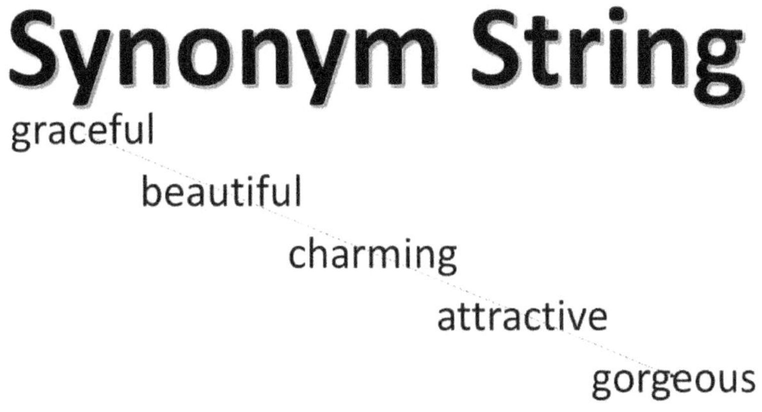

Consider the example in Figure 13. The word *graceful* is being examined through the lens of a simple synonym string. As the words progress, they get more and more positive. One should also notice that the synonyms all relate to physical appearance rather than fluidity of motion. The object of the simple synonym string is to keep the synonyms closely related rather than meandering through gradients of meaning.

More than one option is available for students when beginning a synonym string. For those wanting to compare divergent paths, they can create a dual synonym string like the one in Figure 14. This type of word play allows students to take disparate perspectives of word meanings and see how various permutations continue to alter the interpretations of the terms.

In Figure 14, two prominent synonyms are chosen for the original term *slender*. The top string, based off the synonym *lithe*, has a more positive connotation. The bottom string, based off the synonym *fragile*, takes a more negative view of the starting term. As both strings are extended, students can see how far the two ending terms (i.e., *malleable* and *decrepit*) are from each other.

Finally, a third type of synonym string circles back on itself through many changes in meaning. Starting with the term *sorrow* and moving clockwise (Figure 15), synonyms move from metaphorical descriptions to more physical words (e.g., agony, torture). At the word *pain*, the synonyms start to circle back on themselves and steer away from physical descriptions. The final term *unhappiness* itself is a synonym for *sorrow*, which completes the circular synonym string.

As students work together to create synonym strings, most likely with the help of a thesaurus, they should set out to create one of the specific types of strings. As the strings progress in difficulty, more and more care will have to be given when contemplating word choice. The circular synonym string in particular will take many attempts of trial

Figure 13: Simple synonym string

Figure 14: Dual synonym string

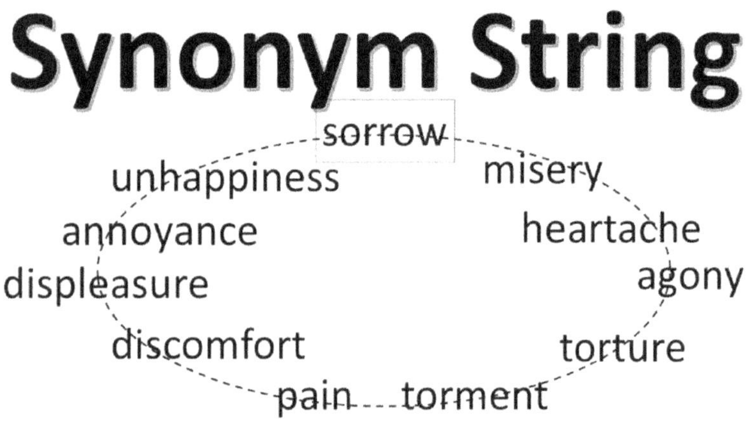

Synonym String

sorrow
unhappiness misery
annoyance heartache
displeasure agony
discomfort torture
pain torment

Figure 15: Circular synonym string

and error before an adequate circle can be formed. By playing with the words as if they were puzzle pieces, students will come to appreciate the power of vocabulary.

In addition to creating synonym strings, students can also work together to dramatically present their strings to the class. For example, after creating a circular synonym string like the one in Figure 15, students then create representations, like charades, of the various words. The goal is not to have students guess the words being demonstrated but to show slight variations as the connotations change.

Starting with *sorrow*, a student might say the word and then stand still with a sad, downcast face. Saying the next word, the student could begin to rub her eyes as if she were crying in *misery*. Moving on to *heartache*, the student could clutch her chest and look longingly into the distance. This continues until the demonstration returns to the original word.

Word riddles

Word riddles are simple questions than have pun-like responses. While they generally cause groans because of the over-the-top word manipulation of their questions and answers, students can create their own to demonstrate a deep and flexible use of language. One way to make word riddles is to choose a subject and generate a list of related terms. For example, if students are working with the subject of *pets*, some examples are *dog, cat*, and *hamster.*

Students then take the first letter off a related term (e.g., *cat*) and list words that begin with that letter cluster. Taking the *c* off *cat*, some words that start with *at-* are *atlas, attitude, attic,* and *athlete*. Then, putting the *c* back onto the new words, punny answers are created – *catlas, cattitude, cattic,* and *cathlete*. All that remains is to make up a riddle for the newly created terms.

Riddle: Where does a pet look when it wants to find maps of foreign countries?

Answer: In a catlas!

Riddle: How do you describe a feline that is always angry?

Answer: It has a bad cattitude!

Riddle: In which part of the house do pets love to play?

Answer: In the cattic!

Riddle: What do you call a pet that loves sports?

Answer: A cathlete!

Another type of word riddle students can create is based of rhyming patterns. Choosing a target word, such as *rustle*, students then list some words that rhyme with it (e.g., *bustle, hustle, muscle, tussle*). The goal is to create questions for which the answers will be the target word and a rhyming word paired together.

Riddle: What do you call it when someone moves quickly and makes soft noises?

Answer: A rustle bustle!

Riddle: What do you call it when you cheat someone in a quiet voice?

Answer: A rustle hustle!

Riddle: What do you call it when a bodybuilder in a tight-fitting nylon jacket flexes?

Answer: A muscle rustle!

Riddle: What do you call it when two brothers are quietly fighting?

Answer: A rustle tussle!

Categories

Remember that vocabulary words are taught not just to improve a student's lexicon but also to increase general knowledge. To that end, students can work alone or with a partner to fill in a simple grid based on a topic and a vocabulary word.

Using the word *graceful*, the teacher might want to focus on character emotions. Students could draw a simple grid with the rows containing the topics and the columns representing the starting letter for each box.

Categories

	G	R	A	C	E	F	U	L
Words that show happiness	glad				enjoy			lively
Words that show anger		rage	animosity	cross		fury		loathing
Words that show patience		relaxed		calm	endure	fortitude	unhurried	
Words that show shame	guilt	remorse	abashed		embarrass			

Figure 16: Categories

What is shown in Figure 16 is a sample of what students might come up with if working together to fill in the cells based on the clues in the first column and the letters of *graceful*. For this type of word play, it would be preferable for students not to use other resources such as a dictionary or thesaurus. Instead, they should pull from their own experiences and prior knowledge to complete the grid in the allotted time (e.g., three minutes).

Experienced teachers might foresee that this type of word play is open to many types of errors. What if students misapply a word? The culmination of this activity is a group discussion. Each team shares their words for each cell and the class, led by the teacher, evaluates and judges the worthiness of the words. If a group has a satisfactory word in a category that no other group could fill, they get 5 points. Otherwise, they get 3 points for categories filled by other groups if the words are unique and 2 points for categories that have a word repeated from another group.

The goal is not to compete, though that will surely motivate many students to get creative with their choice of words. Instead, the conversation about word selection and the justifications that students give are where the real learning takes place. For teachers that want to offer choice without creating competition, students could create their own tables and choose a word to place at the top. The categories in the first column would be the same but students could select a word (e.g., *crevice, pensive*) to use instead of every group using the same word.

Word fluency

Word fluency asks students to generate as many synonyms or antonyms as possible within a given amount of time. This activity can either be accomplished individually or with a partner. Students can repeat this process multiple times choosing different initial letters. If they want to keep score, they can assign one point for each word.

Word Fluency

Word	Synonym
slender	slim
rustle	stir
persecute	struggle
sorrow	sadness
disagreeable	surly
despise	shun
graceful	supple
joyful	satisfied

Word	Antonym
slender	strong
rustle	silence
persecute	soothe
sorrow	satisfaction
disagreeable	sweet
despise	savor
graceful	stiff
joyful	sad

Figure 17: Word fluency

Figure 17 shows various vocabulary words in the first column and either synonyms or antonyms in the second column. The goal is list words that all start with the same letter (e.g., the letter *s*). While the example shows a completed example of both types, it would be better for students to begin with either synonyms or antonyms rather than both.

Regarding the letters to use for generating synonyms or antonyms, students should be directed to start with *s* as it is the most common initial letter in the English language. Following that, the next most common letters are *p*, *c*, *d*, *m*, and *a*. While it might be possible to use other letters with word fluency, it becomes increasingly difficult as the initial letters become less common.

Use these pages to play with words using any of the vocabulary words listed below. Try your hand at synonym strings, word riddles, categories, or even word fluency.

<u>Word bank</u>

commence	*crevice*	*ewer*	*impotent*	*glisten*
muslin	*ominous*	*pensive*	*slatternly*	*sundry*

Notes

Notes

Notes

7 Plan

You have now experienced the five parts of a powerful vocabulary program! In chapter 2 you prepared for instruction, choosing the highest-leverage words to focus on. Next, in chapter 3, you explored how to present new words using the ABCs of vocabulary instruction. Following that, you experienced some techniques in chapter 4 that students can use to place new words within existing semantic domains. Chapter 5 followed that up with a plethora of processing activities, both basic tasks that can be categorized using the four major learning styles (i.e., mastery, understanding, interpersonal, and self-expressive) and complex tasks that incorporate all four styles. Finally, you played with words in chapter 6 with a multitude of methods, including classic games and word manipulation. Now it's time to plan on how to incorporate these various parts into your vocabulary instruction.

Logistics

A topic to consider when contemplating the complexity of a powerful vocabulary program is scheduling. How can teachers of all subjects find the necessary time to encourage students to play with words without sacrificing time dedicated to core content instruction? Even this question is a bit misleading. Time spent on vocabulary instruction serves to bolster general instruction because well-chosen words encompass the main components of the content. Advancing word knowledge supports general learning.

Several scheduling options exist for carving out time for students to wrestle with words. While some experts advocate three minutes each day for five days a week, that small amount of time would restrict many students from diving deep. Instead of a simplistic formula, each teacher must make decisions based on his/her grade level and teaching schedule. If teachers can devote five to ten minutes a day for three or four days a week, that should be more than enough time for students to engage in vocabulary work without dominating the schedule.

Primary grades

For teachers in primary grades, typically considered grades K-2, the use of centers is most likely already in place. Many language arts blocks include literacy centers, comprised of a variety of centers or stations for students to rotate through, including a word work station. This encompasses several components, ranging from learning the alphabet and letter sounds to grammar and vocabulary work. Depending on the level and instructional needs of the students, many parts of a powerful vocabulary program can be easily integrated into a word work station.

Centers sometimes extend beyond the language arts block. Many schools are moving toward working with stations in mathematics instruction. Since vocabulary words encompass knowledge, they can and should be wrestled with across all content areas. Mathematics especially is rich in content-specific terms that students must learn to gain greater computational dexterity.

A common method for math stations uses the acronym STACK, which stands for small groups, technology, apply, create, and kinesthetic. Even if a specific vocabulary station doesn't fit into the established rotation, many of the word play activities would work well in the kinesthetic station. Additionally, some processing tasks would fit nicely with the create station.

Sample schedules

For teachers not in self-contained classrooms, time is of the essence. With some having as little as 45 minutes each day, carving out instructional time for vocabulary instruction can be daunting. The key principle to keep in mind when dealing with limited time is efficiency. How can teachers get the biggest bang for their buck without sacrificing precious minutes?

One solution would be to designate the first few minutes of each class to word work. Sometimes known as a bell ringer, teachers can maximize learning time by developing an entry routine for students. If students know that they have a learning task required of them from the time they come into the room, and if that task just happens to be fun, they'll be much more likely to come in and work right away. This will also help with tardiness since the activity will be designed to be brief but intense.

Proposed schedules will change based on how often a teacher wishes to engage in dedicated vocabulary work. Table 5 shows a variety of routines based on 3-day or 4-day schedules. Committing to a 5-day schedule is extremely difficult to maintain throughout the year. Friday is a great day to catch up on delays encountered throughout the week. Also, enough Monday or Friday holidays are scattered throughout the school year to drive the 5-day devotees nuts.

One part of a powerful vocabulary program, however, does not show up in the sample schedules in Table 5. Presenting new words should naturally exist within the flow of traditional teaching. As teachers encounter words through shared or guided reading, the best time to provide descriptive definitions or other parts of the ABCs of vocabulary instruction is when the words are read or heard in their natural context. If students first encounter word meanings on their own without teacher guidance (e.g., during bell work), they sometimes lack have difficulty seeking additional clarification.

When considering a routine, teachers would be encouraged to periodically change things up. There is a distinct but sometimes invisible line between consistency and falling into a rut. Even the most engaging vocabulary strategies will lose their potency if followed religiously for 30 straight weeks.

Implementation should begin with teacher-directed activities in each of the areas until students gain flexibility with each component. As students repeatedly work with a particular facet, such as drawing semantic maps or playing charades, teachers can begin to provide students with choices. If they have worked with several strategies within a part of the vocabulary program, they can eventually choose how they want to play or process their vocabulary words for that week.

Table 5: Sample schedules

	Monday	Tuesday	Wednesday	Thursday
3-day (1)		Prepare (student choice)	Place	Process (basic or complex)
3-day (2)		Place	Process (basic)	Process (complex)
3-day (3)		Place	Process (basic or complex)	Play
4-day (1)	Prepare (student choice)	Place	Process (basic or complex)	Play
4-day (2)	Place	Process (basic)	Process (complex)	Play

Implementation

Use the following pages to plan how you can integrate the five parts of a powerful vocabulary program into your schedule.

My schedule

The questions below can serve as a guide to evaluate your instructional setting.

- How many days a week would I like to use vocabulary instruction?
- How many minutes per day can I dedicate to vocabulary instruction?
- During what part of the class would students wrestle with words (e.g., centers, bell work, language arts block, etc.)?
- How does my current schedule need to be modified to make this happen?
- How will I introduce the various parts of the program?

_____

_____

_____

_____

_____

_____

_____

_____

_____

_____

_____

_____

Chapter 6 excerpt continued (Jane Eyre)

The play-hour in the evening I thought the pleasantest fraction of the day at Lowood: the bit of bread, the draught of coffee swallowed at five o'clock had revived vitality, if it had not satisfied hunger: the long restraint of the day was slackened; the schoolroom felt warmer than in the morning--its fires being allowed to burn a little more brightly, to supply, in some measure, the place of candles, not yet introduced: the ruddy gloaming, the licensed uproar, the confusion of many voices gave one a welcome sense of liberty.

On the evening of the day on which I had seen Miss Scatcherd flog her pupil, Burns, I wandered as usual among the forms and tables and laughing groups without a companion, yet not feeling lonely: when I passed the windows, I now and then lifted a blind, and looked out; it snowed fast, a drift was already forming against the lower panes; putting my ear close to the window, I could distinguish from the gleeful tumult within, the disconsolate moan of the wind outside.

Probably, if I had lately left a good home and kind parents, this would have been the hour when I should most keenly have regretted the separation; that wind would then have saddened my heart; this obscure chaos would have disturbed my peace! as it was, I derived from both a strange excitement, and reckless and feverish, I wished the wind to howl more wildly, the gloom to deepen to darkness, and the confusion to rise to clamour.

Jumping over forms, and creeping under tables, I made my way to one of the fire-places; there, kneeling by the high wire fender, I found Burns, absorbed, silent, abstracted from all round her by the companionship of a book, which she read by the dim glare of the embers.

"Is it still 'Rasselas'?" I asked, coming behind her.

"Yes," she said, "and I have just finished it."

And in five minutes more she shut it up. I was glad of this. "Now," thought I, "I can perhaps get her to talk." I sat down by her on the floor.

"What is your name besides Burns?"

"Helen."

"Do you come a long way from here?"

"I come from a place farther north, quite on the borders of Scotland."

"Will you ever go back?"

"I hope so; but nobody can be sure of the future."

"You must wish to leave Lowood?"

"No! why should I? I was sent to Lowood to get an education; and it would be of no use going away until I have attained that object."

"But that teacher, Miss Scatcherd, is so cruel to you?"

"Cruel? Not at all! She is severe: she dislikes my faults."

"And if I were in your place I should dislike her; I should resist her. If she struck me with that rod, I should get it from her hand; I should break it under her nose."

"Probably you would do nothing of the sort: but if you did, Mr. Brocklehurst would expel you from the school; that would be a great grief to your relations. It is far better to endure patiently a smart which nobody feels but yourself, than to commit a hasty action whose evil consequences will extend to all connected with you; and besides, the Bible bids us return good for evil."

"But then it seems disgraceful to be flogged, and to be sent to stand in the middle of a room full of people; and you are such a great girl: I am far younger than you, and I could not bear it."

"Yet it would be your duty to bear it, if you could not avoid it: it is weak and silly to say you CANNOT BEAR what it is your fate to be required to bear."

I heard her with wonder: I could not comprehend this doctrine of endurance; and still less could I understand or sympathise with the forbearance she expressed for her chastiser. Still I felt that Helen Burns considered things by a light invisible to my eyes. I suspected she might be right and I wrong; but I would not ponder the matter deeply; like Felix, I put it off to a more convenient season. (Public Domain)

Prepare

Using your own judgment, the 4-quadrant vocabulary (chapter 2), or a combination of both, select the words that are useful and/or important for students to wrestle with.

Present

Apply the ABCs of vocabulary instruction (chapter 3) to some or all of the words you chose. Plan out how you want to present them to students (e.g., during instruction, before the lesson begins, after reading, etc.).

Place

Select one or two tasks for students to place words within context (chapter 4). Will students select which words to place or will that be teacher-controlled?

Process (basic)

Select at least one activity from each learning style (chapter 5) that students can use to process vocabulary words. Will any tasks need to be created beforehand?

Process (complex)

Select at least one complex processing task (chapter 5) that students can participate in to showcase the depth of their vocabulary knowledge. Will any exemplars need to be made for students to use as a reference?

Play

Choose some ways for students to play with words (chapter 6). Remember that these activities serve not only to reinforce current learning but also are a great vehicle for reviewing previously learned terms.

Planning Matrix

	Monday	Tuesday
Prepare		
Present		
Place		
Process		
Play		

Planning Matrix

Wednesday	Thursday	Friday

Planning Matrix

	Monday	Tuesday
Prepare		
Present		
Place		
Process		
Play		

Planning Matrix

Wednesday	Thursday	Friday

Notes

Notes

Notes

Now that you've spent time wrestling with these ten words, rate them again using the word knowledge scale (chapter 2). After you've reassessed your knowledge of each word from a scale of 1 to 4, compare your new ratings to your original ratings (chapter 2).

Word	New Rating	Original Rating	Word	New Rating	Original Rating
commence			muslin		
crevice			ominous		
ewer			pensive		
impotent			slatternly		
glisten			sundry		

What parts of a powerful vocabulary program do you find most useful? Which parts do you need more support with? Which parts can you use immediately?

_____

_____

_____

_____

_____

_____

_____

_____

About the Author

Aaron lives in Ft. Worth, TX, with his wife Heather, his children Dave, Drew, Desiree, and Daniel. He is an avid disc golfer and sports nut, closely following the Rangers, Cowboys, and Mavericks. He enjoys fantasy novels, Star Trek: The Next Generation, the Marvel Cinematic Universe, and reading peer-reviewed educational psychology research articles.

Before becoming an education consultant, Aaron spent 11 years in the classroom as a 3rd, 4th, and 6th grade teacher. He also spent several years as a campus and district administrator of a charter school in Arlington, TX.

If you would like to learn more about one- and two-day training options for schools and districts, visit him online at AaronDaffern.com. You can also email him at AaronDaffern@gmail.com.